DELUXE EDITION

HOW TO DRAW THE CUTEST STUFF!

union
square
kids

NEW YORK

THIS BOOK BELONGS TO:

....

....

DELUXE EDITION

HOW TO DRAW THE CUTEST STUFF!

Angela Nguyen

union
square
kids

NEW YORK

union
square
kids

NEW YORK

UNION SQUARE KIDS and the distinctive
Union Square Kids logo are trademarks of
Union Square & Co.

Union Square & Co., LLC, is a subsidiary
of Sterling Publishing Co., Inc.

© 2022 Quarto Publishing plc

ISBN 978-1-4549-4656-4

For information about custom editions,
special sales, and premium and corporate
purchases, please contact
specialsales@unionsquareandco.com.

Printed in China

2 4 6 8 10 9 7 5 3 1

06/22

unionsquareandco.com

MIX
Paper from
responsible sources
FSC® C169965

Contents

Chapter one
PEOPLE 18

Chapter two
FOOD & DRINKS 44

ENTER PLANET CUTE

DRAWING AND COLORING ARE SO MUCH FUN, and you can use your imagination to make lots of wonderful pictures. This book contains step-by-step drawings to add cute-appeal to anything and everything, from animals and food, to transportation, people, and lots more.

There are also interactive pages, along with fun activities with each picture. Explore, count objects, add your own cute drawings, and make up stories. Do this on your own or ask a grown-up for help.

You'll find stickers on the last four pages of the book and a poster within an envelope. The sticker sheets are easy to tear out and take with you. Feel free to add the stickers wherever you want—in this book, in your notebooks and journals, or even on the poster!

You can use colored pencils, felt-tip pens, or markers to color in the pictures.

The beginning of each chapter shows all the projects you can choose from. Just pick the one you like best and get going.

Need a bookmark? You'll find two cute ones on the book's front flap. Cut around the dotted lines (ask an adult for help). The animals can save your place in the book!

Chapter three
ANIMALS

This chapter is packed with a menagerie of adorable animals, from cats and dogs to birds, fish, and kangaroos.

HAMSTER 74 · CATS 75 · DOGS 76 · BUGS 78 · GIRAFFE 80

DEER 91 · SLOTH 92 · COLORFUL BIRDS 93 · FISH 94 · PENGUIN 96

ALPACA 81 · BIG CATS 82 · BEAR 84 · KANGAROO 86 · KOALA 87

OTTER 97 · WALRUS 98 · BAT 100 · HORSE 101 · SHARK 102

RABBIT 88 · HEDGEHOG 89 · MOOSE 90

DOLPHIN 103 · OCTOPUS & SQUID 104 · TURTLE 105

Slip the back cover flap beneath your chosen activity page to protect the picture on the next page.

Ice Cream

Instead of a cone, a popsicle has a stick.

These popsicles are perfect for any summer's day.

Ice cream with a swirl starts with a circle, but add a shark-fin shape on top.

Draw in the swirls around the circle and add the animal features.

This ice cream has swirls of chocolate and vanilla.

This is a really easy starting point: a circle on top of a triangle.

Draw in the animal details. This one is a seal.

Color in the seal and the lines for the waffle cone.

1. Color this page in with your favorite pencils.
2. Color in the Neapolitan ice cream cone in the top corner—that's a scoop of chocolate, vanilla, and strawberry.
3. Color the macaroni in different colors—what flavors are these?

Complete the activities and then color them in. When using colored pencils, vary how much you press down with the tip of the pencil to make the color darker or lighter.

GETTING STARTED

You don't need any special tools or materials to start drawing cute stuff. Experiment with different pens, pencils, and surfaces, and learn how to give your drawings cute appeal!

TOOLS AND SURFACES

There are many types of tools you can use to draw and color cute stuff. These are some of the tools that I love to use.

You can pick up any piece of paper and draw a creature on it.

Try not to drop colored pencils because the lead inside will break.

How cute is this unicorn pencil topper?

Crayons

If you're going to be doing a lot of coloring, crayons can be a fun tool to play with. They make interesting textures and thick strokes.

The #2 pencil is a go-to!

PENCILS

Pencils are ideal for sketching and creating fun textures. Pencil marks are also easy to erase.

Surfaces

You don't need special paper; any kind of drawing surface is just fine. If you want to keep all your drawings together, you could use a sketchbook, or a simple notebook.

Sticky notes are fun to draw on. You can stick them anywhere and everywhere!

There's no going back with a pen.

MARKERS

Markers can be risky because they are ink-heavy, so test them out first. I have some markers in my office that are light and create beautiful thick lines.

PENS

These are my favorite! Pens are great when you want a thin line. You can get precise markings, perfect facial expressions, or pattern details.

Sharpies define lines.

Use art markers for rich color and vibrancy.

START WITH SHAPES

The world is full of amazing things that you can draw using just a few basic shapes.

THE THREE YOU KNOW

Let's start with a circle, a triangle, and a square. Each shape can be drawn longer, skinnier, fatter, larger, or smaller to create other shapes.

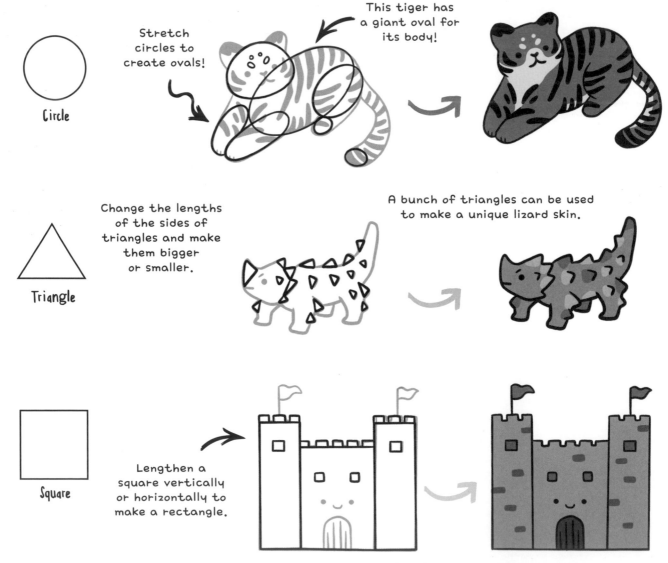

Circle

Stretch circles to create ovals!

This tiger has a giant oval for its body!

Triangle

Change the lengths of the sides of triangles and make them bigger or smaller.

A bunch of triangles can be used to make a unique lizard skin.

Square

Lengthen a square vertically or horizontally to make a rectangle.

A lot of buildings are made up of squares and rectangles.

SPECIAL SHAPES

Now let's look at three special shapes that will come in handy.

Blob

A blob is drawn using squiggly lines.

Squiggly blobs make up the foliage of a Japanese bonsai tree.

Jelly bean

Check out this big jelly bean.

The jelly-bean shape is my favorite to draw! It is mostly used for the bodies of animals.

Gumdrop

You can make some fun creatures with this shape.

Gumdrops are a good shape to try out.

ANIMALS ALIVE

Action lines are special effects you can add alongside your animals to animate them. Bring your animals to life!

Try a dotted path to show where your animal is walking.

Small curved lines create simple movement effects.

Curved lines can show that your animal is happily bouncing along.

Draw straight lines coming out from the face. Surprise!

Wavy lines are most effective for underwater creatures. You can show which direction this stingray is swimming!

You can add all sorts of fun special effects, like hearts, sparkles, or sleepy "z"s.

Straight lines give this tiger speed!

You can tell this dog is wagging its tail because of the small curved lines I drew.

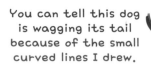

EXPRESSIONS

By changing facial expressions and adding action lines
next to your creatures, you can give life to your beasts
and clearly communicate how they are feeling.

HAPPY
A simple, happy face!

FUNNY
A smile and
upward eyebrows.

ANGRY
A frowny face,
slanted eyebrows,
and a puff of steam.

SAD
Upward eyebrows
and an upside-down
mouth.

SCARED
Upward eyebrows,
open mouth with
extra lines, and water
droplet symbols.

MISCHIEVOUS
Crooked eyebrows
and a bold smile.

SURPRISED
Open mouth, lifted
eyebrows, and
expression lines.

DANGEROUSLY CUTE
One tooth poking out.

BORED
Straight eyebrows
and a slanted mouth.

PLAYFUL
Closed eyes and tongue
sticking out.

WORRIED
Upward eyebrows
with a frowny face.

BASHFUL
Upward eyebrows, a
blush, and a heart.

KEEP IT CUTE

Now that you know the basics of drawing with shapes,
here are some extra, easy-to-use tips to help
you make sure what you draw is always cute.

Notice the difference between a realistic
and a cute drawing of the same dog.
Simpler shapes and less detail are key.

SIMPLIFY

The most important step when making cute drawings is to simplify what you draw by using less detail. Keep to the basic shapes so your drawing can focus on being cute.

Sharp lines

Lots of detail

This is the Sydney Opera House in Australia.
I drew it using lots of lines and details.

We can make it cuter by simplifying the
shapes and rounding the lines. There are no
complicated details, but there is a face, and
musical notes have been added!

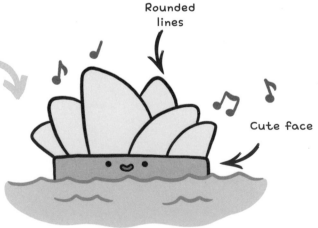

Rounded lines

Cute face

FACES
Add a cute face to anything you draw to transform it into an adorable character!

Take this bagel, for example . . .

. . . simply add a face and ears to the bun and you have your first animal-food fusion.

COLORS
Dark and dull colors make your drawing look very serious. Light, pastel, or bright colors give cute drawings a soft touch.

Add a face to the ice cream . . .

. . . or the cone

ROUNDED LINES
Take away sharp features and add roundness to your drawings to make them cuter. Just like chubby features on a baby or a puppy!

Chapter one
PEOPLE

Drawing cute people requires features to distinguish them, and accessories and clothes to decorate them. In this chapter, I'll show you how to bring all sorts of characters to life!

Heads & Bodies

PROPORTIONS

Two-and-a-half circles make a basic figure.

PERSPECTIVE

I like to use horizontal and vertical lines to help me draw people turned in different directions. The horizontal line is where the eyes and nose rest. The vertical line is the center of the person's face.

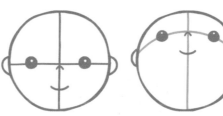
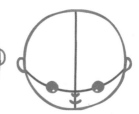

If you draw the horizontal line higher, your person will be looking up.

Move the horizontal line lower and your person will be looking down.

HAIRSTYLES

There are so many different hairstyles you can give your character. Hairstyles can also make your person look more like a boy or a girl.

Put some clothes on and
then you've got a person.

You can add eyelashes to
make your person more
feminine.

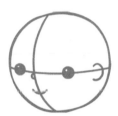
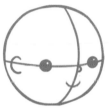
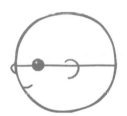
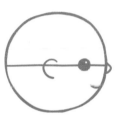

If you draw the
vertical line to
the left, your
person will be
looking left.

Move the vertical
line to the right
and your person
will be looking
right.

Poses

Try some of these poses!

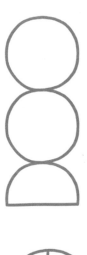

Remember: a person is made of two-and-a-half circles.

Add some lines to show that the leg is moving quickly. What a kick!

Changing the angle of the feet can help with the gesture. Try making your person tiptoe.

Accessories

Fuzzy hats are fun to draw and wear.

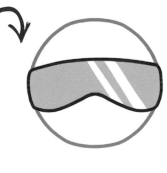

This is how I keep my head warm in the winter.

Some glasses have one lens and go across the whole face.

Don't forget that you can change the shape too.

Chef

Draw wavy lines coming from the plate to show the delicious scent.

Master chef is a master egg flipper! Add lines from the pan to the egg for movement.

Police Officer

Deck your character out with an equipment belt and cool shades.

Astronaut

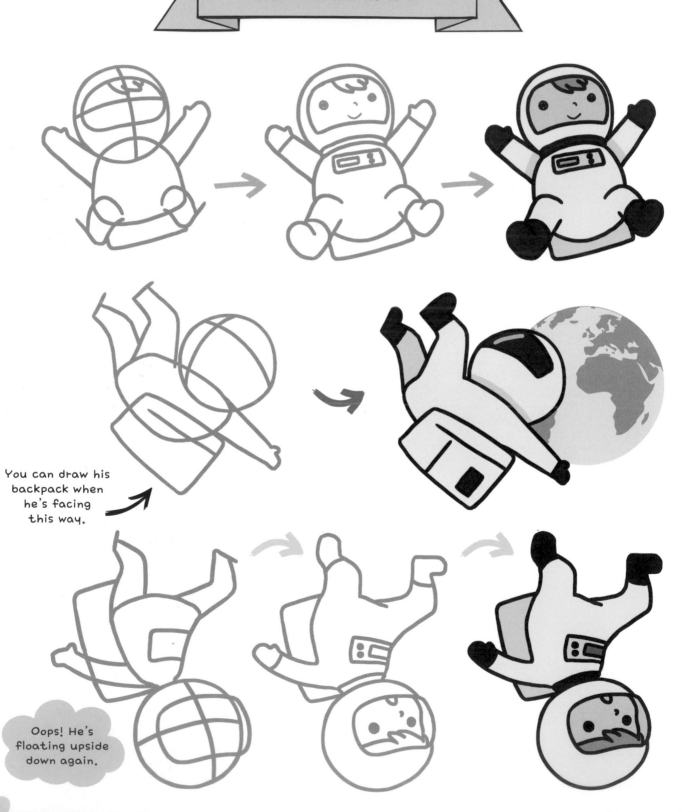

You can draw his backpack when he's facing this way.

Oops! He's floating upside down again.

1. Color this page in with your favorite pencils.
2. How many different planets can you spot? Give each one a name.
3. Two of the astronauts are floating upside down. Do you know why?
4. Create your own flag design for the astronaut to hold. It can be for a made-up country or planet.

Sailor

Give your sailor a telescope so he can see farther.

X Marks the spot.

You can draw your own treasure map.

Lifeguard

Start your lifeguard with the base of a person and include one arm and leg.

Lifeguards patrol the beaches to keep people safe.

Add the other arm and leg. The second leg is bent to show the lifeguard is running.

Continue adding details like the hat and surfboard.

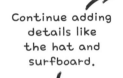

Finish the drawing with the details on the clothing and hair.

Beach umbrella

Sun hat

Basket

Beach chair

Farmer

Yum! Add a bite mark to the apple the farmer is eating.

Keep the crops growing! Give your farmer a watering can.

1. Color this page in with your favorite pencils.
2. This boy is busy gardening. Draw a pair of gardening gloves to keep his hands clean.
3. Count the ladybugs and then add some more.
4. What else does the boy need to look after the flowers? Look at the previous page for a clue.

Flamenco Dancer

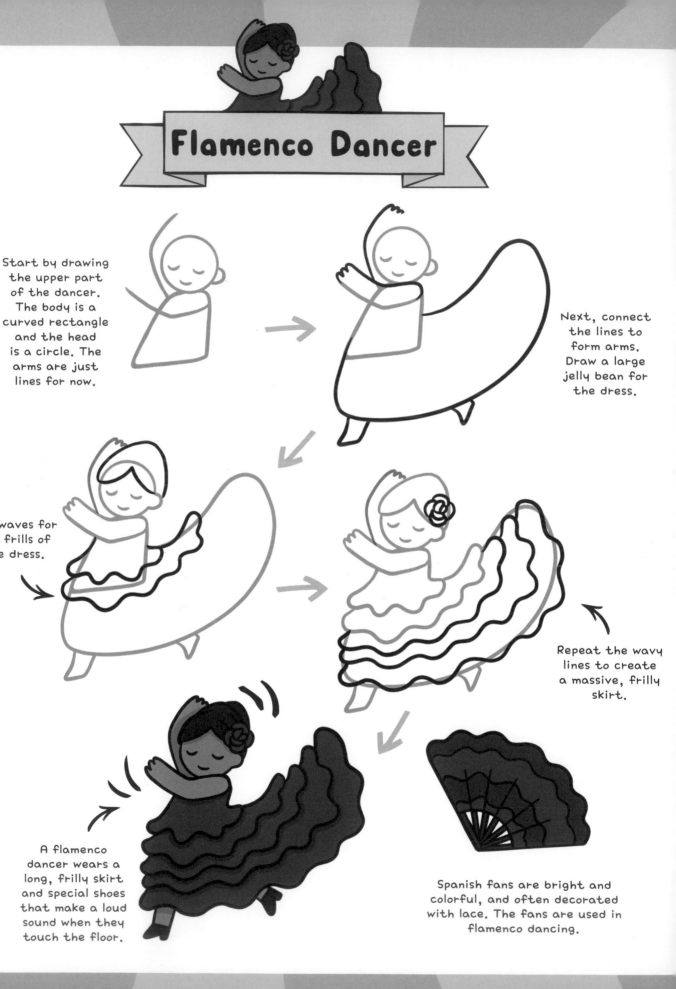

Start by drawing the upper part of the dancer. The body is a curved rectangle and the head is a circle. The arms are just lines for now.

Next, connect the lines to form arms. Draw a large jelly bean for the dress.

Add waves for the frills of the dress.

Repeat the wavy lines to create a massive, frilly skirt.

A flamenco dancer wears a long, frilly skirt and special shoes that make a loud sound when they touch the floor.

Spanish fans are bright and colorful, and often decorated with lace. The fans are used in flamenco dancing.

Samurai

Begin with a circle and gumdrop. This will be the body and head of your samurai.

. . . then start the helmet and sword.

Add the arms and legs . . .

Imagine the armor as a group of rectangles. Add them on top of the body.

Finish off with stripe patterns on the armor.

Ninja

Draw your ninja right-side up and then turn your paper upside down.

1. Color this page in with your favorite pencils.
2. What do you think the ninja on the left is using to stay upside down? Rope? Peanut butter? Write five good and bad ideas on this page.
3. Draw different patterns on the ninjas' masks.

Cowhands

Cowboys are so cool! This expression can be drawn with closed eyes and a smirky smile.

Did you know that cowhands herd cattle?

The cowgirl and her lasso can be drawn with ovals.

Musicians

Balalaika

Accordion

Begin by drawing the base of a person.

Add a large triangle on top of your person; this is where the balalaika will be.

Bring the player to life with a face and arm, and add the neck to the balalaika.

Finish with the details of your player's hair and clothes, and add the strings and tuning keys to the instrument.

Day of the Dead

Draw a jelly bean on top of the head; this will be the hat.

Day of the Dead is a Mexican celebration where families remember their ancestors. The holiday is very colorful and decorative.

Draw the base of a person, using a circle and rectangles.

Add a peanut shape to start the cello.

Now for the tricky parts: the details! Add these to the outfit and the cello one at a time.

Continue drawing details, like the pattern of the hat and the colors on the face. Draw in the strings of the cello.

K-pop Band

Korean pop, or K-pop, is fun music performed by young and talented artists. It is popular with young people.

When drawing a K-pop band, think of cool poses for your group!

Draw the base of your people . . .

. . . then add fun clothing. Group clothing doesn't have to match.

Add musical notes around your band.

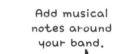

Sometimes Korean bands will make stuffed animals that are based on them. This cat has the same colors as one of the band member's hair!

At concerts, fans will bring signs and glow sticks to wave!

Witch

You can make a cute witch by giving her a big hat and a simple dress.

A successful potion! Draw a green aroma coming out of the glass.

1. Color this page in with your favorite pencils.
2. The witch is taking off on her broomstick—
   draw a cat to sit at the end of the long handle.
3. How many stars can you see with the same
   pattern?

Traditional Dress

To draw the traditional Vietnamese áo dài, begin with the base of a person.

Add the tunic and the hat.

Lastly, draw on the designs of your tunic! You can choose anything from flowers, to animals, to patterns.

Draw the base of a person with their arms outward.

On top of the base, draw a triangular hat. Add the details of the clothing too.

Continue drawing in details, such as the sides of the hat, the face and the body.

The Dutch traditional costume includes simple pinafores, trousers, and pointed hats.

Add small sparkles, triangles, and dots to make a detailed dress.

Draw the base of a person using a circle and two gumdrops.

Draw on the person's face and their arms. Imagine the arms are rectangles.

Add a sash that can drape over the shoulder and arm.

Add the final part of the sari over the other arm, then color in the outfit.

Loose clothing is multipurpose: it can cover your entire body but still be light! It also protects you from the sun and lets the wind breeze through.

To protect themselves from the sun, people in Morocco cover their heads with hats and scarves. Some may also cover their heads for religious reasons.

Chapter two
FOOD AND DRINKS

HOT DOGS

46

CHIPS

47

HAMBURGER

48

BREAD

49

NOODLES

50

TACOS

51

SUSHI

52

DUMPLINGS

53

PIZZA

54

COTTON CANDY

56

POPCORN

57

BREAKFAST FOODS

58

In this chapter you might find cute animals swimming around in your noodles or wrapped up in a cozy tortilla.

FRUIT

60

PIES

62

MACARONS

63

ICE CREAM

64

JUICE

66

MILKSHAKES

67

FANCY FIZZIES

68

TEA

70

COFFEE

71

Hot Dogs

Every hot dog starts with a cylinder. Save the top circle for the face.

Draw the bun in at the sides, as if it's hugging the dog, and add ears and a face.

Add legs and a tail for a comfy, chilled-out hot dog!

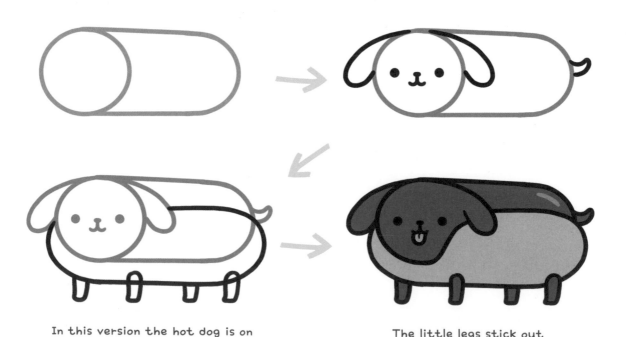

In this version the hot dog is on all four legs. Instead of drawing a vertical cylinder, draw a horizontal one.

The little legs stick out from the bun, so that this hot dog can run and play.

The base of a
simple potato chip
is a curved oval.

Draw on a face
and ears.

Perfect! A bunny
potato chip.

Some chips look
more puffy than
others!

Use the entire chip
as a face or a body.

You can decorate a chip
bag any way you please.

Try making the entire
bag an animal,
like this one.

Or the animal can
be part of the
packaging design.

47

Hamburger

Start at the top of
the hamburger by
drawing a bun and
some cheese.

Pop some round
ears on top of the
bun, then add the
burger, lettuce,
and the bottom bun.

Draw in the animal
face and color the
hamburger.

This time, add legs
and a tail to the
top bun, as well as a
face and ears.

Draw the rest of
the burger as if
your animal is laying
on top of it!

The top bun
can be used
to illustrate
any kind of
animal.

The trick is how
you draw the ears.
Try ears that point
up or droop down.

Bread

Draw a square and
two circles.

Draw a puddle around the
butter to make It melt on
the toast.

Bread is usually bought in
loaves like this.

These bread buns
are like bundles
of circles.

Baguettes can be
large or small.

Noodles

The size of your bowl
will determine how
many ingredients you
can fit into it.

Give wavy noodles a try!
Repeat this pattern to
fill the bowl.

Add a bunny egg on
top of your noodles.

Start with the bowl
and bear—or any
other animal!

Draw the noodles
around and over your
cute creature.

Noodles are great for
wrapping around your
animal.

Tacos

Start with the head and paws of your animal . . .

. . . then add the taco shell so that the animal is laying inside it. Give your animal a face too.

Add your choice of foody toppings and fillings.

Start with the taco shell, then add a face and ears.

Now add the yummy fillings. I like meat tacos with red tomatoes, yellow cheese, and green lettuce.

You could make the taco a part of your animal, like this cat's body. See how its legs and tail stick out from the shell.

A burrito is a rolled-up tortilla. When drawing animal burritos, imagine a creature all wrapped up in a blanket!

Sushi

The key to most sushi drawings is starting with round shapes such as circles and cylinders.

Add your animal on top. I chose a cat.

Add a rectangle for the seaweed wrap.

Now imagine how your animal will lie.

Dumplings

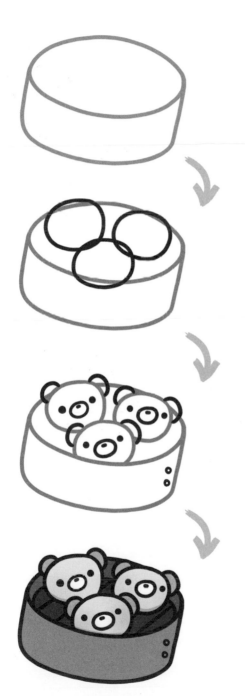

Add in the details and finishing touches.

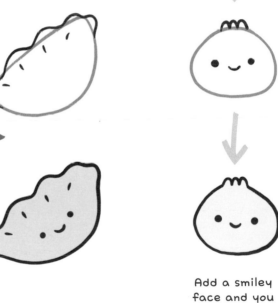

Check out how I added crease lines to the bun where the chopsticks pinch it. Ouch! It really looks like the soft bun is being pulled.

Add a smiley face and you have a cute little bao bun!

Pizza

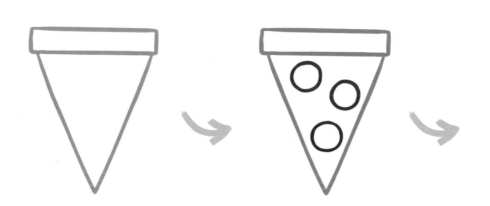 

Create your animal by giving the pizza crust a face and ears.

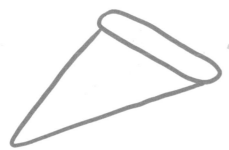 

One of my favorite things about pizza is how cheesy and melted you can make it look.

These cute little chicks make the perfect pizza partner!

What's your favorite topping?

Peppers

Olives

Pepperoni

Mushrooms

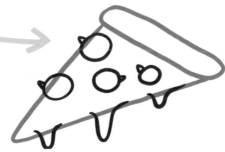

1. Color this page in with your favorite pencils.
2. Draw some of your favorite toppings on the pizza—
   there are mushrooms, tomatoes, peppers . . .
3. Draw some cute faces on the fries and pizza slices.

Cotton Candy

Draw three wide ovals for the body of your cotton candy.

Draw a larger, more exaggerated triangle for cotton candy that is about to be eaten.

Cotton candy comes in all kinds of shapes. Don't be afraid to make it tall!

Drawing the face on the cone instead of the body makes the candy look like hair!

Choose three cute colors for a bag of cotton candy.

Popcorn

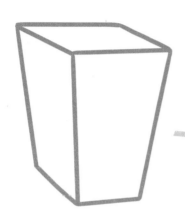

This is a typical popcorn bag you might buy at the movies. The base is like a tall box.

Draw on the face, ears, and limbs of your animal.

Then add in the striped colors and popcorn filling.

Draw your animal on the bag itself. It looks like a cute packaging design!

Color the popcorn brown if you like the chocolate flavor.

Breakfast foods

Draw the toast base and circular shapes for the egg.

Add ears and a face to the yolk for a cute animal egg-on-toast meal.

I like to think of crepes as a triangle bed.

Add circles with ears to the top of the bed (these are the animals' heads).

Finish with the details and decorate your crepe with chocolate syrup.

You can pick your own fruit. My favorites are blueberries and raspberries.

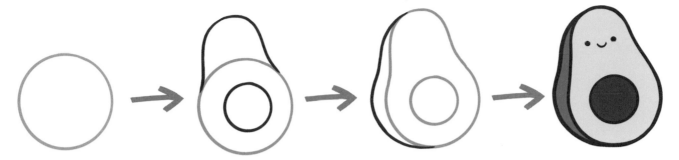

Mexico produces the most avocados in the world! Start by drawing a circle.

Draw a smaller circle inside; this will be the pit. Add a hill shape at the top to form the shape of an avocado.

Finish with a cute smiley face.

An omelet is made using whisked eggs. This dish is less oozy, so the shape can be drawn with straight lines.

Add some bacon.

Draw a face in the middle part of the omelet and add ears on top.

Crack out an oozing creature.

The round yolks of over-easy eggs make the perfect shape for animal faces.

Bacon is the perfect egg companion.

Fruit

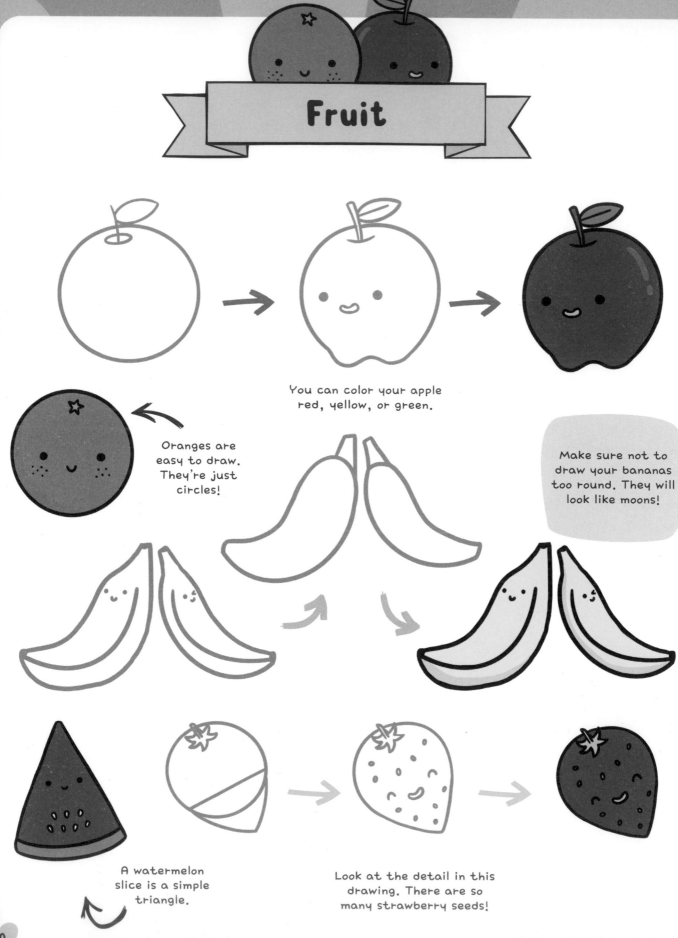

You can color your apple red, yellow, or green.

Oranges are easy to draw. They're just circles!

Make sure not to draw your bananas too round. They will look like moons!

A watermelon slice is a simple triangle.

Look at the detail in this drawing. There are so many strawberry seeds!

1. Color this page in with your favorite pencils.
2. How many types of fruit can you see on the platter?
3. Draw some more blueberries on the stalk—don't forget to add their faces!
4. What do you think the slice of melon is saying to the strawberry? Write this in the speech bubble.

Pies

The base of this pie is a semicircle and rounded rectangle.

Add a wavy line for the pastry frill and an animal sleeping on top.

Notice how the cat is a similar shape to the pie. They're both round and cute.

Start with a base made of simple lines.

Draw the animal face and ears on your base. Draw a wavy line for the bottom of the pastry.

Here's a dog pie face!

So that we can see the whole of the pie top, this time draw a full oval and the wavy pastry line.

An animal can pop out of the center of the pie.

Draw little bits of pie flying out from the sides to make the drawing really pop.

Macarons

Any macaron can be drawn with these three steps. Step 1: Make the buns.

Step 2: Add the filling to the center.

Step 3: Color in the macaron. Now you're ready to add animal faces!

 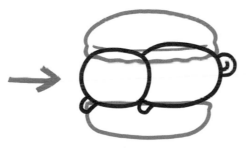 

Begin with the top and bottom buns.

The filling is the animal. Add a circle for the head and body, then limbs and a tail.

Add in the details and you've got yourself a doggy macaron.

Mint-green frog

Lilac kitty

Chocolate poppy

Colorful unicorn

Instead of a cone, a popsicle has a stick.

These popsicles are perfect for any summer's day.

Ice cream with a swirl! starts with a circle, but add a shark-fin shape on top.

Draw in the swirls around the circle and add the animal features.

Draw in the swirls around the circle and add the animal features.

This ice cream has swirls of chocolate and vanilla.

This is a really easy starting point: a circle on top of a triangle.

Draw in the animal details. This one is a seal.

Color in the seal and the lines for the waffle cone.

1. Color this page in with your favorite pencils.
2. Color in the Neapolitan ice cream cone in the top corner—that's a scoop of chocolate, vanilla, and strawberry.
3. Color the macarons in different colors—what flavors are these?

Juice

A juice box kind of looks like a small house.

Draw in a bent straw to complete the juice-box look.

This last part is up to you. What flavor do you want to color your juice box?

Pineapple cat

Peach deer

Grape bunny

Juice boxes come in many shapes and sizes. You can draw your animal on the box or make the box itself into an animal, like this monkey.

Milkshakes

Turn any mug into an animal! Imagine having a mug and then adding the head, limbs, and tail.

Start drawing frosting with a semicircle, then add in the curvy lines on top.

There are various ways to add animals to milkshakes. The animal could be on top, floating inside, or even the cup itself.

This is a candy stick poking out of the milkshake!

The whipped cream on top of this milkshake has been turned into a wooly dog.

Fancy Fizzies

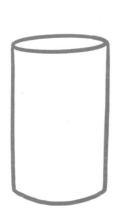

Draw the base shape of a seal inside the glass. Add a circle to the edge for the fruit decoration.

Color in your glass of fruit juice. This is a refreshing pineapple juice for a hot day.

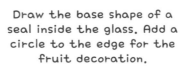

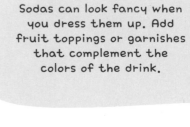

Sodas can look fancy when you dress them up. Add fruit toppings or garnishes that complement the colors of the drink.

This time, add a triangle on the edge of the glass for a watermelon garnish.

Color in the drawing with bright pink colors and add the details to the watermelon slice.

Look at this fun striped straw!

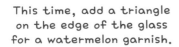

1. Color this page in with your favorite pencils.
2. Draw a straw in the tumbler glass, so the little animal standing on the lemon slice can take a sip.
3. Add a pattern to the pretty parasol and some cool shades for the animal chilling in the soda.
4. Milkshake, ice cream sundae, or soda—find your favorite treat, then draw a happy face on the glass or bowl.

Tea

Let's draw a fancy teacup. Remember to make it curvy.

Add in the dainty details, such as floral designs or little curved lines.

The final touch is a little animal relaxing in the warm drink.

Bubble tea is a combination of milk and tea.

Bubble tea contains chewy additions called boba.

The boba can be given animal features.

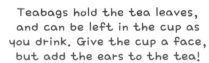

Teabags hold the tea leaves, and can be left in the cup as you drink. Give the cup a face, but add the ears to the tea!

Coffee

Add ice inside the container and foam on top of the coffee.

Give the foam animal features and add caramel sauce and a straw.

Latte art is a creative way to add animals to coffee.

Draw a take-out coffee cup.

Add a sleeve around the cup. This protects you from the hot contents.

Color in your cute animal sleeve and coffee cup.

Chapter three
ANIMALS

HAMSTER

74

CATS

75

DOGS

76

BUGS

78

GIRAFFE

80

ALPACA

81

BIG CATS

82

BEAR

84

KANGAROO

86

KOALA

87

RABBIT

88

HEDGEHOG

89

MOOSE

90

This chapter is packed with a menagerie of adorable animals, from cats and dogs to birds, fish, and kangaroos.

DEER

91

SLOTH

92

COLORFUL BIRDS

93

FISH

94

PENGUIN

96

OTTER

97

WALRUS

98

BAT

100

HORSE

101

SHARK

102

DOLPHIN

103

OCTOPUS & SQUID

104

TURTLE

105

Hamster

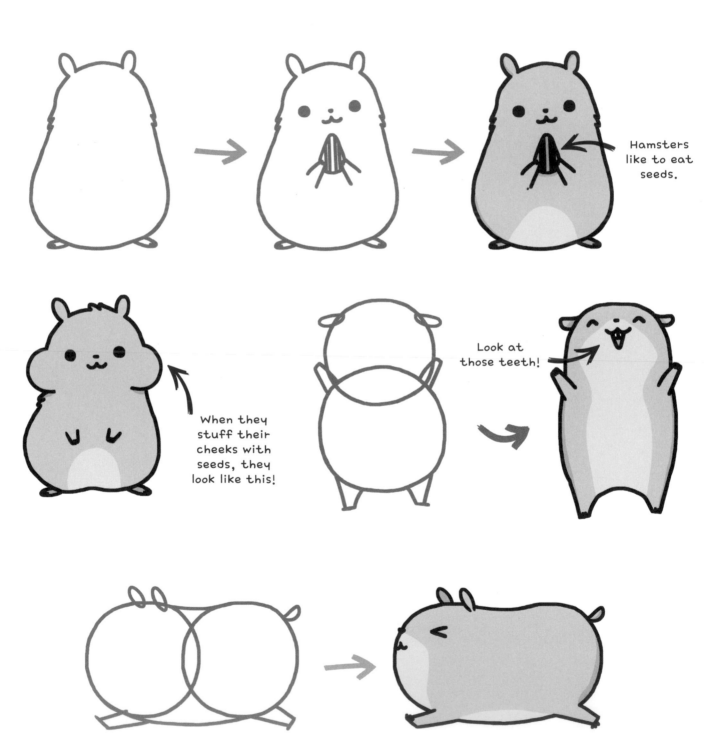

Hamsters like to eat seeds.

When they stuff their cheeks with seeds, they look like this!

Look at those teeth!

74

Cats

There are many things cats like: toys, string, food, catnip, napping, and grooming.

Yarn

Mouse toy

Fish

Catnip

Cats spend a lot of time just laying around.

Dogs

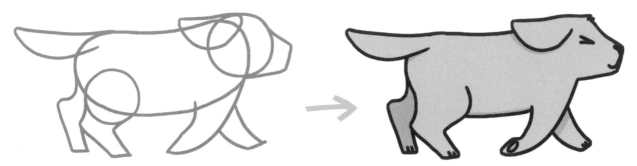

Look at how the dog's legs move.

Check out this dog's wrinkly forehead!

Curl up your dog when it sleeps.

z^zz

Some dogs are hairier than others. Look how fluffy this dog is!

Make your dog's fur flow in the wind when it runs.

The ears you choose for your dog will give it a certain personality. For example, pointy ears make a dog look alert, while droopy ears make a dog look relaxed. See what happens when you draw your dog with these different ear shapes.

Pointed   Curvy   Long   Droopy   Triangular

Bugs

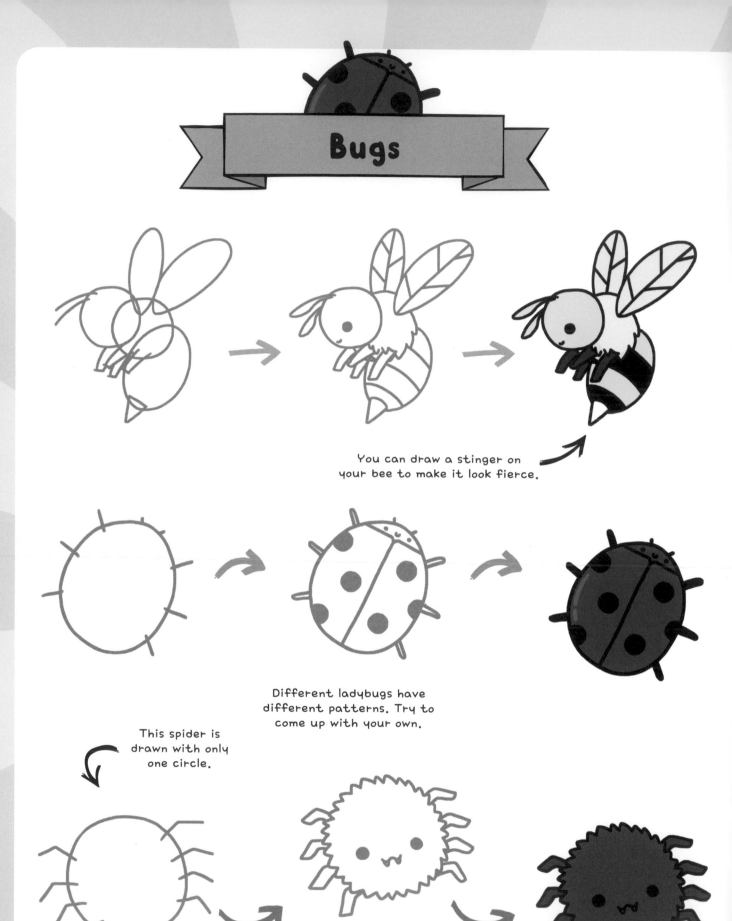

You can draw a stinger on your bee to make it look fierce.

Different ladybugs have different patterns. Try to come up with your own.

This spider is drawn with only one circle.

Grasshoppers can jump and fly.

A butterfly can have many patterns on its back.

Giraffe

Giraffes have long necks so they can reach the delicious leaves high up in the trees.

Draw bending legs to show your giraffe galloping.

Alpaca

The base of the alpaca is made up of many circles and ovals.

On top of the base, draw in tufts of fur. They look like clouds!

Add decorations on the ears.

Draw in accessories like a necklace and a saddlebag.

Color in the accessories with bright colors!

Alpacas have soft, fluffy wool, which people use to make warm clothes. You can color the accessories any way you prefer; I chose red, green, and yellow!

Big Cats

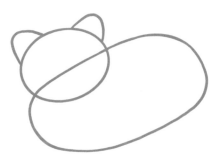

Draw a circle for the head, triangles for the ears, and an oval for the body.

Add the front and back legs. Imagine them as rounded rectangles, with an extra oval connecting the back leg to the body.

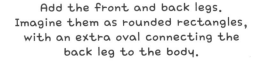

Siberian tiger

Now that you have your tiger, add the stripes! The stripes make a pretty pattern when they are spaced evenly over the body.

The final pattern on the tiger is the light color around its mouth and down its chest.

Begin by drawing a circle for the head, with an oval snout.

The body is like a jelly bean. Add the limbs, tail and face.

For the spots, draw circles, dots, and moon shapes.

Jaguar

Make the base of the lion a cat with floppy ears.

The mane of a lion grows as he matures. To draw a female lion, draw a cat without a mane.

Add the fluffy mane. Imagine making a cloud around the lions head.

Lion

Even the tail is fluffy!

Short mane   Medium mane   Thick mane

Bear

Give your bear a big, round body but little ears!

Bears need a lot of body fat to get them through the hibernating months. Draw a really round bear!

This bear is catching fish in the river. Yummy salmon!

Your choice of color will distinguish which type of bear you are drawing: perhaps a polar bear, a grizzly bear, or a panda? Color your own bears to show what type they are.

Kangaroo

Kangaroos have pouches to hold their babies. Baby kangaroos are called joeys.

Kangaroos can travel long distances by hopping. Draw three hopping symbols to show that your kangaroo is on the move.

Koala

Koalas hop from tree to tree in search of their favorite leaves to munch on.

Koala ears are sooooo soft. When drawing them, give them lovely fluffy edges.

Rabbit

Angry Winking Thinking Surprised

This bunny is happily munching on a tasty carrot snack.

Some bunnies have floppy ears, while others have perky ears.

Hedgehog

There are about 5,000 to 7,000 spikes on a hedgehog, but you don't have to draw that many!

I like to start the hedgehog with a silhouette. Then define where the back and belly are with a line.

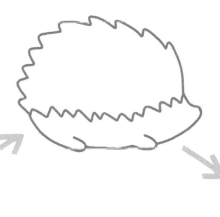

When you draw the belly of a hedgehog, begin with a round shape.

89

Moose

The moose is made up of round shapes. I like to start with the small circular head, and then draw the large oval body.

Add in details like the hanging fur below the neck.

The fur hanging from a moose's neck is called a dewlap.

Once you have added more details to your moose, erase the pencil lines.

When coloring the moose, you will need three colors: a light tan for the antlers, a brown for the fur, and a darker brown for the hooves.

Deer

If you want your deer to have antlers, decide whether they should be short or long.

Short antlers   Long antlers

I like to add patterns on my deers' backs. Make your own set of dots for your deer.

Sloth

Sloths are usually sleepy, but your creations can have all sorts of facial expressions.

Loving

Excited

Sleepy

Sloths use their long claws to hang from tree branches.

Colorful Birds

Birds' beaks vary in shape and size. This toucan has an especially large beak.

Round beak   Small beak

Long beak   Curved beak

Drawing a peacock takes patience: you need to repeat the tail feathers over and over.

This cockatoo has a funny feathered hairdo.

Fish

A sunfish is like a large swimming square!

Goldfish can't close their eyes, even when they sleep.

To draw a puffer fish, draw a round fish and then add spikes.

Patterns can make a fish look difficult to draw. Try drawing the outline first and color in after!

Your choice of color and pattern can change how your fish looks. Here is a school of fish. I've colored some, but the rest are blank for you to complete. You can look at real tropical fish for ideas, or use your imagination to create a whole new species.

Penguin

Penguins like to slide on their tummies! Wheeee!

Want to draw a baby and parent penguin? Start by drawing a small one . . .

. . . then draw another penguin, only bigger this time!

Otter

Draw movement lines around your otter to make it float in water.

Nervous

Shocked

Thinking   Excited

Angry

Your otter can have so many different expressions!

Walrus

Walruses have long teeth called tusks!

It's really easy to add whiskers to your walrus. Just draw a few short straight lines!

This walrus is lying flat on its belly. Tuck its flippers neatly by its side.

Complete this drawing! Give the walrus tusks, whiskers, and flippers. Then color him in and add your choice of background.

Bat

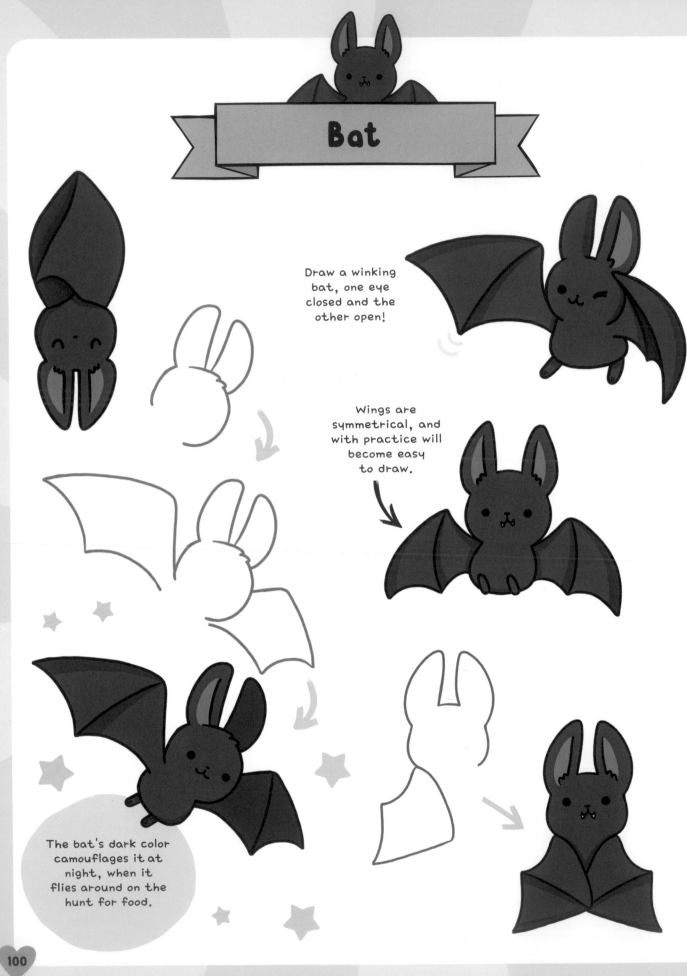

Draw a winking bat, one eye closed and the other open!

Wings are symmetrical, and with practice will become easy to draw.

The bat's dark color camouflages it at night, when it flies around on the hunt for food.

Horse

This horse proudly wears its saddle when carrying humans.

Try out this front angle view of a horse. It looks really speedy when you add motion lines.

The direction of the horse's hair can help show which way it is walking.

Sharks

Pointy teeth and angry eyebrows make a shark look scary.

It is not too surprising that a hammerhead shark has a head that looks like a hammer!

A whale shark has a round, fat body type.

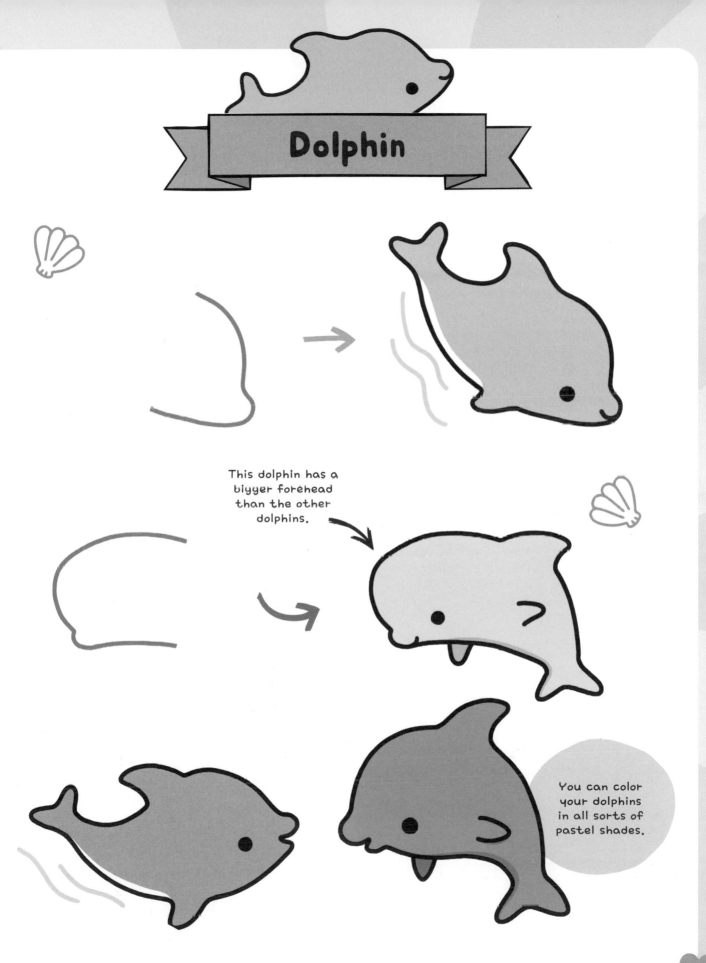

Dolphin

This dolphin has a bigger forehead than the other dolphins.

You can color your dolphins in all sorts of pastel shades.

Octopus & Squid

Their sticky tentacles mean octopuses can cling onto rocks and plants.

Squid are so fun to draw. Begin by drawing their bodies, then add the arms!

Turtle

When drawing turtles, start with the head, then position the shell behind it.

Different shell angles

Try drawing a turtle hiding in its shell. Its eyes are peering out at you!

Turtles like to eat vegetables and fruit.

NESSIE 108

KRAKEN 109

BUNNY OCEANA 110

TENTAGON 111

GHOST WHALE 112

CHINESE DRAGON 113

COSMIC GIRAFFE 114

GRIFFIN 116

SOAREPHANT 117

FLOATING PUFFBALLS 118

HORNED TIGER 119

WEREWOLF 120

FIRE PUPPY 121

UNICORN 122

ROCK FELLA 124

TROLLS 125

OTTREE 126

CELESTIAL CAT 127

DINOSAURS 128

Chapter four
CREATURES

This chapter is packed with mythical, imaginary, and extinct creatures, some you'll recognize and some that will surprise you. But they are all really adorable.

Nessie

Starting with the head and body makes it easier to visualize the rest of the nessie's body.

The direction of the neck determines which way the nessie is facing.

The nessie may be shy, but still enjoys swimming with its little fish friends.

Kraken

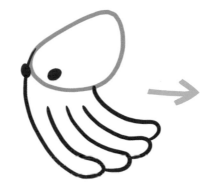

The head is not a regular oval, but is lopsided instead; one end is large while the other end is small.

Check out those suction cups on the inside of the tentacles.

The arms can really inform the emotion of the kraken. This one looks friendly because it's waving!

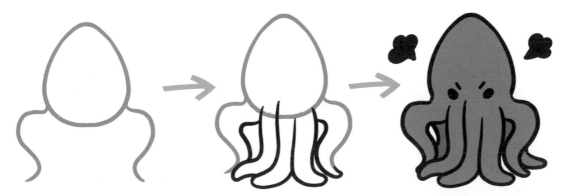

Draw the oval head and start with some lines for the beginnings of the arms.

Continue to draw out the arms. They are bent and look a bit angry.

Add black puffs to show just how angry the kraken is!

Bunny Oceana

When the bunny oceana is swimming, draw its head and body horizontally.

Use the round face and body as a guide to filling in the rest of the features.

When this bunny's arms and tail are up, it's ready to celebrate!

When its ears are halfway down, the bunny is shocked!

Ears up with puff symbols show that it's angry.

Lowered ears with a rain cloud means the bunny oceana is super sad.

Tentagon

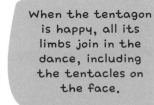

When the tentagon is happy, all its limbs join in the dance, including the tentacles on the face.

You can draw three different wing poses to show the tentagon flying.

When the tentagon is standing up, its body is like an oval.

The wings have a triangular shape to them.

Color the wings slightly darker than the rest of the body.

Ghost Whale

Start the ghost whale by drawing the body. Then slowly add the skeleton.

The skeleton may look difficult, but it's easy you draw the bones one by one.

Chinese Dragon

I always start with a circle for the head. Then connect it to the long body.

Continue expanding the body. Draw the mouth, ears, and front legs.

Add details such as triangular spikes to the dragon's back and tail, and a long horn on its head.

The Chinese dragon is commonly depicted as a snake with four legs. If knowing this helps you to draw your dragon, then just imagine making a snake first!

Cosmic Giraffe

Start with the base of the giraffe. The body is a jelly bean.

Draw in the patterns. They look like wonky squares.

Add in the space outfit! You'll need a circle for the helmet and other details for the suit.

Use dark brown and orange for the giraffe's characteristic pattern.

1. Color this page in with your favorite pencils.
2. Some of the stars are joined up—can you connect more of the stars with lines?
3. The unicorn, sloth, and chicken are playing on the planet's ring. Can you name some planets with rings?

Griffin

To create this cool background, draw a triangle, then overlap it with oval clouds.

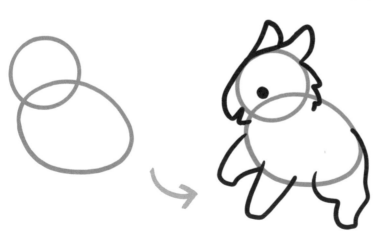

Make a circle head and oval body. Then draw in the limbs and bird's head around the shapes.

The last step is drawing the triangular wings and long tail.

Soarephant

As with most of the creatures you draw, start with circular shapes for the head and body.

Add the ears and limbs, not forgetting the cute trunk.

The wing is like an elongated rectangle, to which you can add feathery details.

Floating Puffballs

Draw dashed lines and color the center of the back detail for a puffy effect.

Some puffballs are smaller than others.

What a big leaf! Sometimes the leaves are even bigger than the puffballs.

This puffball has wings on its back.

. . . for three little plants!

You can also draw the bodies with ovals instead of circles.

This puffball has more than one shape on its back . . .

Horned Tiger

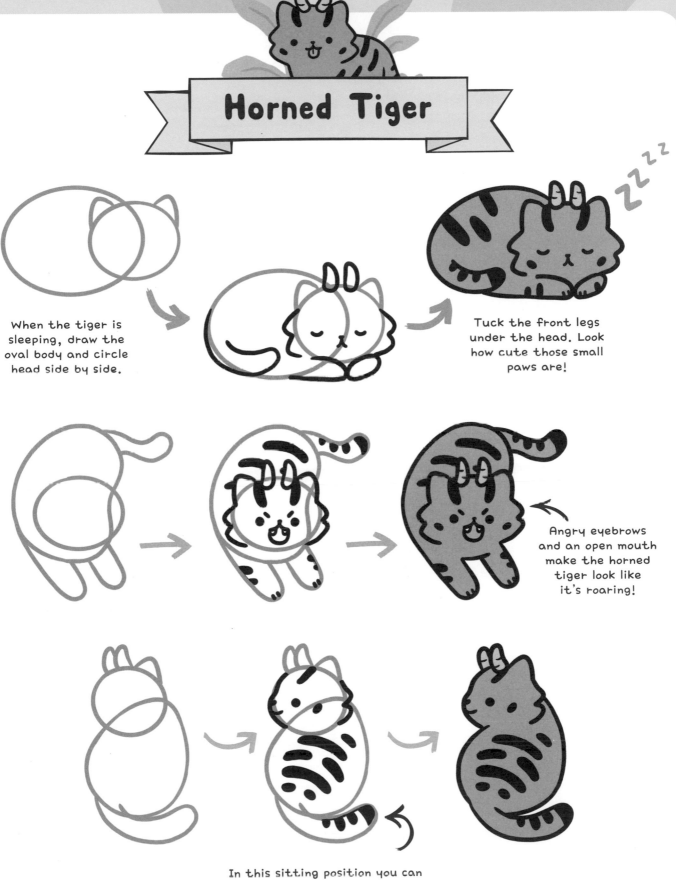

When the tiger is sleeping, draw the oval body and circle head side by side.

Tuck the front legs under the head. Look how cute those small paws are!

Angry eyebrows and an open mouth make the horned tiger look like it's roaring!

In this sitting position you can see all of the tiger's stripes. You can draw any pattern of stripes.

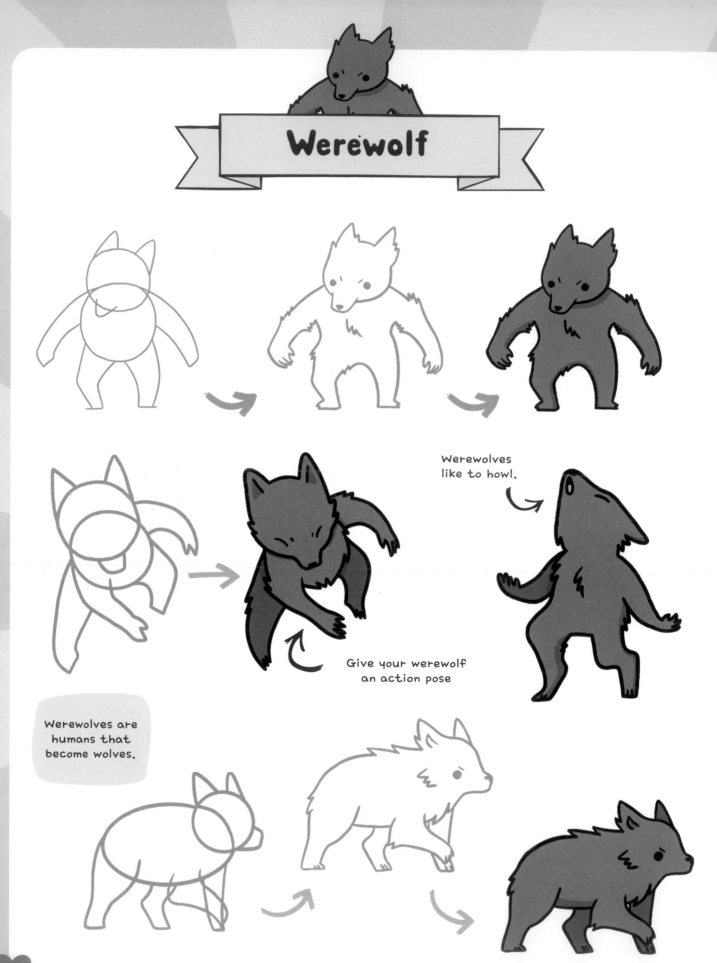

Werewolf

Werewolves like to howl.

Give your werewolf an action pose

Werewolves are humans that become wolves.

Fire Puppy

The fire puppy looks similar to a cat to start with.

Drawing in the snout makes it look less like a cat.

Draw a round snout for the side profile.

Add a wavy shape to the tail and little flames shooting out nearby.

To make the fire puppy look like it's laying down, draw the limbs closer to the body.

Unicorn

Draw the unicorn's mane in the same direction as its neck. The lines for the mane and neck almost run parallel.

To make a dynamic pose, draw the unicorn's head facing its body.

The snout of the unicorn is like a semicircle. Erase any extra lines you don't need later.

1. Color this page in with your favorite pencils.
2. Unicorns are magical creatures and can make wishes come true. Write or draw two wishes in the clouds.
3. There are lots of stars twinkling in the picture, but can you count how many eight-pointed stars there are?
4. Draw a pair of wings for the starry unicorn, so he can soar through the air with his friend.

Rock Fella

Adding little details like small lines and boulder marks really adds character to your rock fella.

The key to drawing rocks is to make round shapes more rigid, so add straight lines around your initial ovals.

The legs are like small, soft rectangles. Top off the head with moss and plants.

Trolls

Every troll begins with a simple shape. The tree troll starts with a gumdrop.

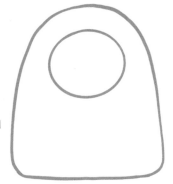

Draw jagged shapes around the gumdrop. Imagine these are messy leaves.

Draw two triangular trees on top of its head.

Add more jagged lines to turn the triangles into trees.

The rock troll has a hexagonal shape.

The mountain troll has a triangular shape.

125

Ottree

Color in the ottree with a bright brown for the fur and a forest green for the leaves.

Draw leaves all the way down the ottree's spine.

Draw a circle for the face and a jelly bean for the body. Add a couple of ears.

Add the front paws and a tail to the jelly bean.

Celestial Cat

Add sparkles around your three-eyed cat to make it look mysterious and celestial.

The cat's head is like a horizontal oval, while the body is more of a vertical oval.

Cat poses are fun to draw because they are made of wavy lines, like the limbs and tail.

Dinosaurs

Show your pterodactyl's flight path with dashed lines.

Pterodactyls are flying dinosaurs.

A triceratops has a funny fan-shaped head and three horns on its face.

Quick! Draw a running T-rex. Use lines to show how fast it's going!

The dinosaurs on this page are herbivores, meaning they like to eat plants. Draw plants around them so they have something to snack on throughout the day and night.

Chapter five
TRANSPORTATION

This chapter is packed with cute things that fly, float, and travel across land to take you from one place to another.

Space Stuff

Three, two, one, blast off!

Add fire for effect.

Draw a UFO in space or on Earth.

On the Road

Vroom vroom!

Here's a profile of a car.

You can draw a vehicle's face on the window.

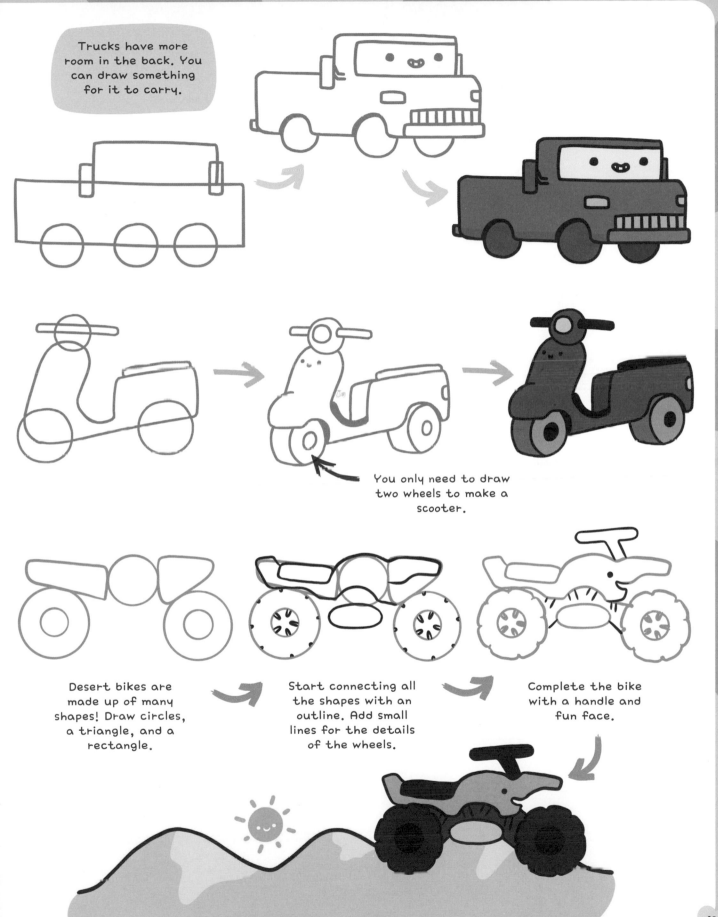

Trucks have more room in the back. You can draw something for it to carry.

You only need to draw two wheels to make a scooter.

Desert bikes are made up of many shapes! Draw circles, a triangle, and a rectangle.

Start connecting all the shapes with an outline. Add small lines for the details of the wheels.

Complete the bike with a handle and fun face.

All Aboard

Add this submarine to your underwater illustrations.

A cruise ship is a giant boat! Draw a small boat for comparison.

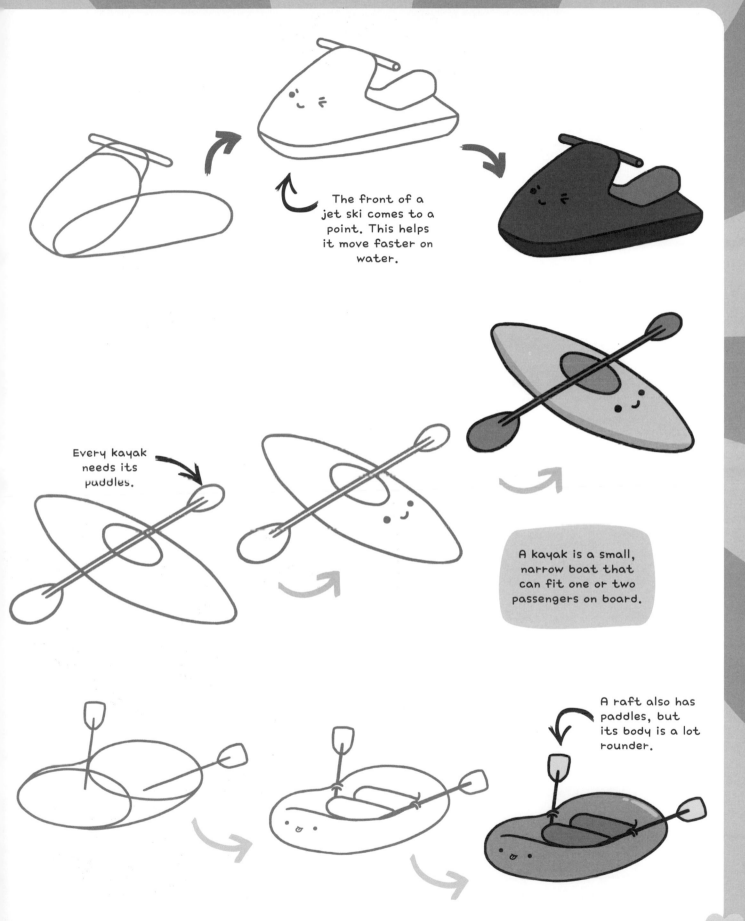

The front of a jet ski comes to a point. This helps it move faster on water.

Every kayak needs its paddles.

A kayak is a small, narrow boat that can fit one or two passengers on board.

A raft also has paddles, but its body is a lot rounder.

Take Off

Draw this plane among the clouds!

Jets are faster than planes. Their bodies are a little sharper and thinner.

Unlike the airplane, the helicopter's propeller is on the top.

This plane has a silly nose.

1. Color this page in with your favorite pencils.
2. There are lots of ways to get around, but what is missing from this picture?
3. How many ways of transportation use the sea, rivers, and lakes? And can you point out the ones that travel by land?
4. Draw a flag on top of the boat's mast and add a cool design.

CHAIRS 140

TABLES 141

COOKING TOOLS 142

TEAPOT 144

TELESCOPE 145

RUBIK'S CUBE 146

BEAUTY PRODUCTS 147

HOUSES 148

SKYSCRAPERS 149

FARM BUILDINGS 150

VOLCANO & CACTI 151

TREES 152

HANGING PLANTS 153

CROPS 154

FLOWERS 155

SPRING 156

SUMMER 157

FALL 158

WINTER 159

Chapter Six
MORE CUTE STUFF

Everything can be cute! This chapter focuses on inanimate objects, from chairs to cooking tools and everything in between!

Chairs

Give the sofa some pillow friends by drawing squares.

A sofa chair is like the sofa cut in half.

Make the bottom curved so the chair can rock.

Tables

Decoration on a table can make it look more fancy.

Tables can have faces on the top or side.

The face of this table is on the side!

Add clothing to your table to give it some personality.

Cooking Tools

Most cooking tools have long handles.

Oh no, I'm melting!

The fatter you make the bag, the more icing it has!

Measuring cups come in families.

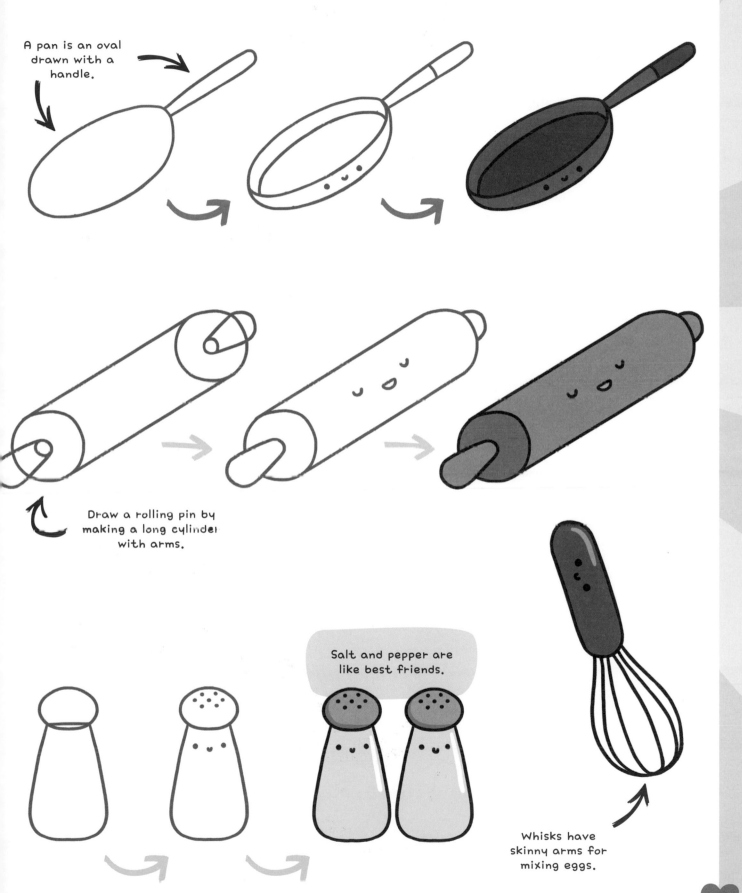

A pan is an oval drawn with a handle.

Draw a rolling pin by making a long cylinder with arms.

Salt and pepper are like best friends.

Whisks have skinny arms for mixing eggs.

Teapot

Try drawing a teapot and teacup set. Start the pot with a circle.

Extend the spout of the pot and add the curved handle and also a supporting base and lid. It's starting to look like an elephant.

Add the facial features. Now it looks like a happy, cute elephant.

Add a small teacup to pour your hot tea into. Now you have a set.

Telescope

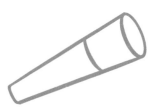

To draw a small
telescope, make
a cylinder.

Stargazing is a popular
activity in Chile because the
deserts have clear and open
skies. The largest telescopes
(bigger than the Statue of
Liberty) are in Chile!

Add the telescope
stand by creating
a triangle at
the bottom.

Draw more lines
for the stand and
start erasing the
extra lines.

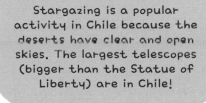

There are four telescopes
called The Very Large
Telescopes. They look like
these boxes.

Draw a planet!

Rubik's Cube

Draw a slanted square.

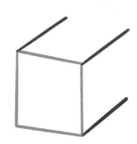

Draw three diagonal lines coming out from the corners. Make sure these lines are all the same length.

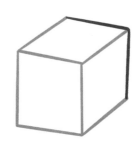

Close off the cube by connecting the diagonal lines.

Draw two connected lines on the top and on the side of the cube.

Draw another two lines on the top and front.

Add two lines to the front and side of the cube, and a smiley face.

This colorful puzzle was invented by Erno Rubik, who is Hungarian.

Beauty Products

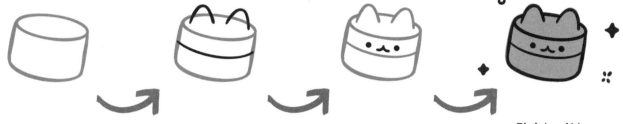

Let's draw a small lip gloss container by starting with a cylinder.

Add the cap line and some cat ears.

Finish with a face and sparkles!

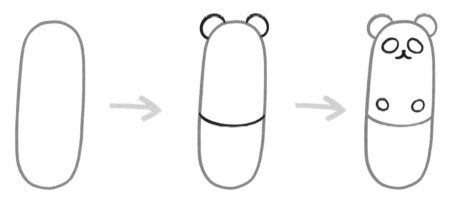

Begin with an oval.

Add panda ears . . .

. . . and a face, and hands.

Drawing lipstick can be cute when you add a panda face!

Open the cap to reveal the lipstick!

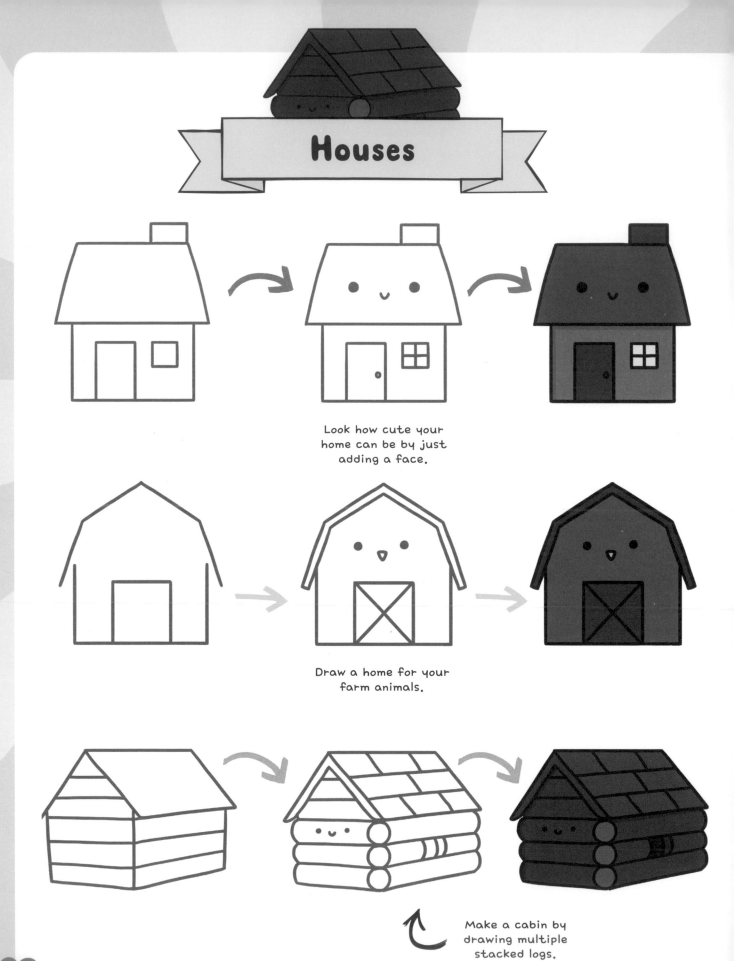

Houses

Look how cute your home can be by just adding a face.

Draw a home for your farm animals.

Make a cabin by drawing multiple stacked logs.

Skyscrapers

A skyscraper is a very tall building. It can simply be drawn with a long rectangle.

You can make this skyscraper by drawing more than one rectangle.

Some skyscrapers are pointier than others!

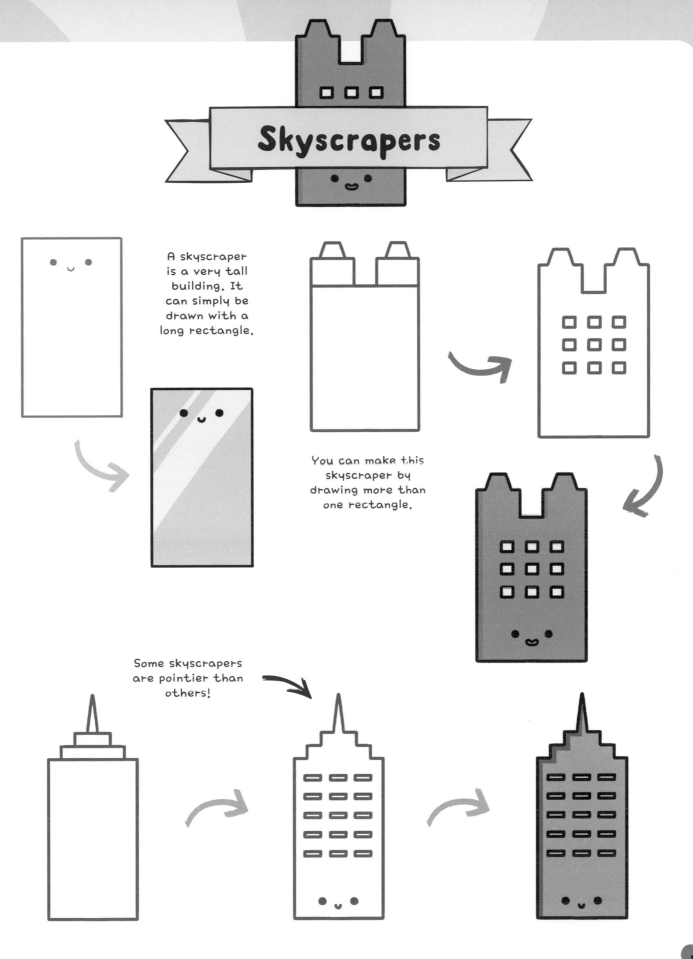

Farm Buildings

A greenhouse is where you can keep your plants.

Create a rectangle below the gumdrop. For the blades, draw an "X." Add a little rectangle for the door.

Draw rectangles at the ends of the "X" and finish with a cute face.

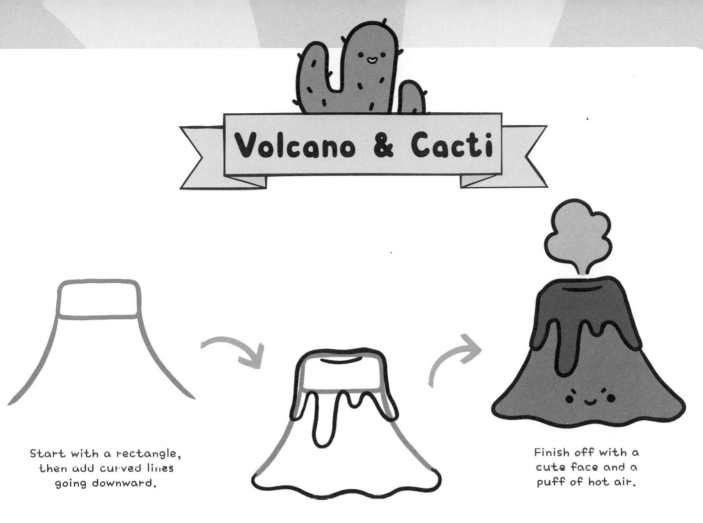

Volcano & Cacti

Start with a rectangle, then add curved lines going downward.

Draw oozing lava on top of the rectangular base.

Finish off with a cute face and a puff of hot air.

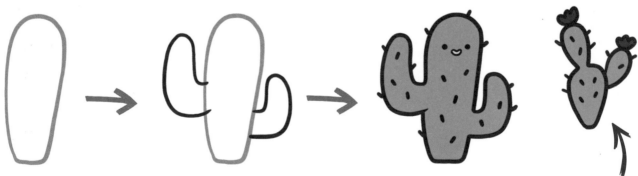

You can draw cactus plants in several ways. This cactus is upright with two arms.

Add little prickly lines when you've completed the shape.

Some cacti are smaller, fatter, and have flowers.

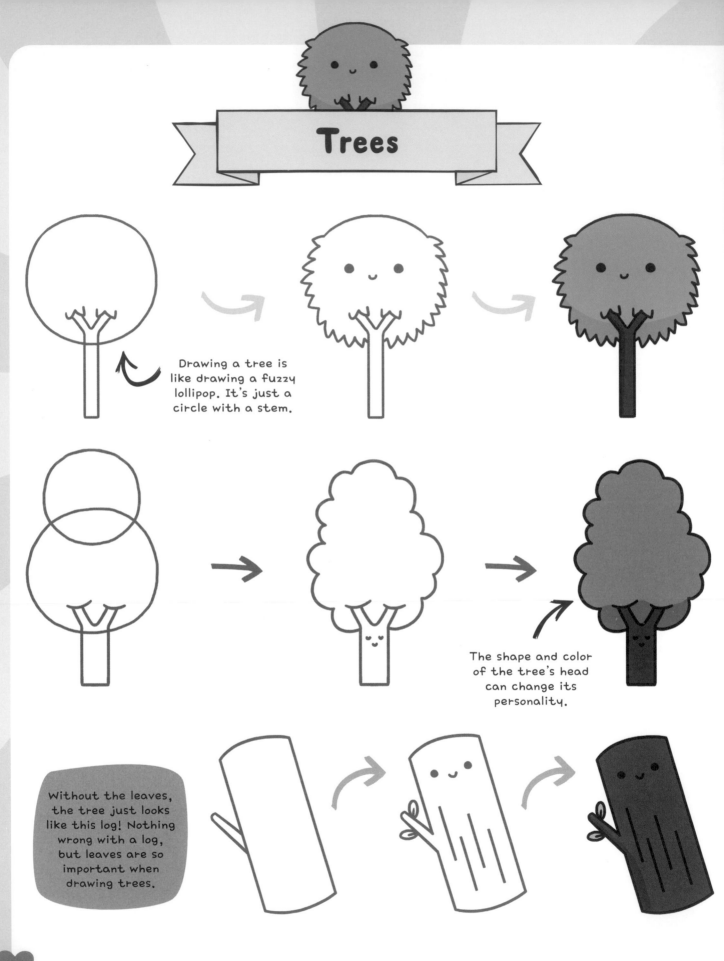

Trees

Drawing a tree is like drawing a fuzzy lollipop. It's just a circle with a stem.

The shape and color of the tree's head can change its personality.

Without the leaves, the tree just looks like this log! Nothing wrong with a log, but leaves are so important when drawing trees.

Hanging Baskets

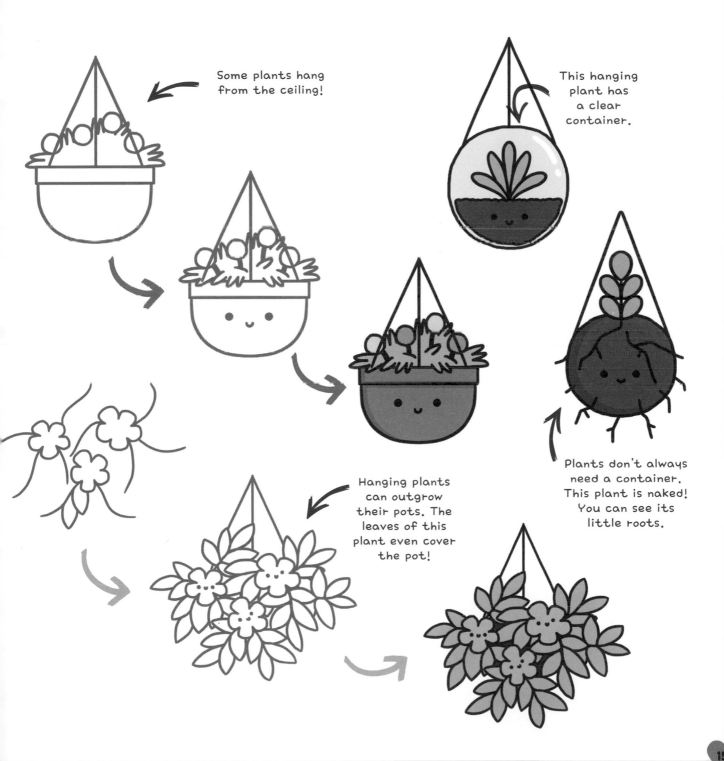

Some plants hang from the ceiling!

This hanging plant has a clear container.

Plants don't always need a container. This plant is naked! You can see its little roots.

Hanging plants can outgrow their pots. The leaves of this plant even cover the pot!

Crops

This cute teddy bear is stuffed with cotton.

Egyptian cotton is handpicked and super soft. Cotton is used to make clothing and toy stuffing.

Draw three circles with stems coming out of the bottom.

Draw clouds around the circles to form the cotton. These are called cotton bolls.

Give them all cute faces!

Draw lines sticking out on the sides.

Start drawing the bamboo by making a skinny rectangle.

Draw on leaves and add horizontal lines to the stem.

Flowers

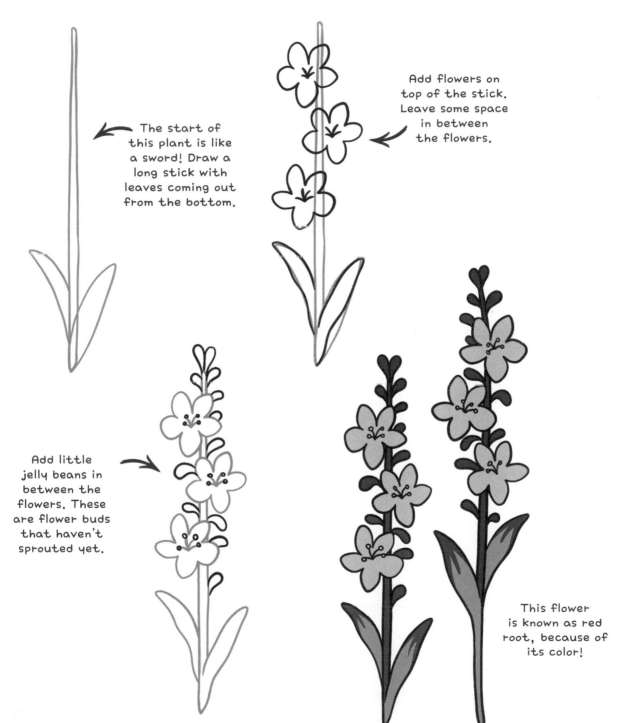

The start of this plant is like a sword! Draw a long stick with leaves coming out from the bottom.

Add flowers on top of the stick. Leave some space in between the flowers.

Add little jelly beans in between the flowers. These are flower buds that haven't sprouted yet.

This flower is known as red root, because of its color!

Spring

Tulips are made of a circle and triangles.

A sunflower consists of one large circle and small half circles.

Draw many flowers wrapped together to create a bouquet!

There are so many different types of flowers. The lily has an interesting shape.

Roses are red, violets are blue, this rose can be drawn by you!

Summer

The base of a gelato cone is two circles and a triangle.

Add the dripping gelato to the bottom of the circles.

Finish with faces on the ice cream and diagonal lines down the cone.

This is a cute tent set up by the trees.

Camping in a forest or in the mountains is a fun activity.

When camping in the wilderness, people like to cook their meals on a barbecue.

Fall

For the maple leaf, start with a circle.

Next, add three large leaf sections evenly around the circle. Don't forget to add a stalk!

Keep adding smaller leaf sections in between the large ones you drew.

Maple leaves change color each season. Color your leaves red for autumn or make them green for spring!

A soup is a great place for swimming animals to hang out, like this alligator.

Winter

A pine tree is a big green triangle.

Draw faces on the hockey stick and puck for extra cuteness.

An igloo is easy to draw. Just make a half circle!

In Canada, a tuque is a type of warm hat. Grab a tuque and some gloves to go outside!

Credits

Quarto would like to thank the following Shutterstock contributors
for supplying images for inclusion in this book:

Aleksandr Semenov/Shutterstock.com; Anchalee Ar/Shutterstock.com; Erica
Truex/Shutterstock.com; HappyPictures/Shutterstock.com; KittyVector/
Shutterstock.com; La Gorda/Shutterstock.com; Max Krasnov/Shutterstock.
com; Natthareya/Shutterstock.com; Oakview Studios/Shutterstock.
com; Oleh Svetiukha/Shutterstock.com; Paper Wings/Shutterstock.com;
Sudowoodo/Shutterstock.com; Tanya K/Shutterstock.com; tunejadez/
Shutterstock.com; Vetreno/Shutterstock.com.